WEATHER AROUND YOU
SUNSHINE

Anita Ganeri

WEEKLY WR READER®
EARLY LEARNING LIBRARY

Please visit our web site at: www.earlyliteracy.cc
For a free color catalog describing Weekly Reader® Early Learning Library's list
of high-quality books, call 1-877-445-5824 (USA) or 1-800-387-3178 (Canada).
Weekly Reader® Early Learning Library's fax: (414) 336-0164.

Library of Congress Cataloging-in-Publication Data

Ganeri, Anita, 1961-
 Sunshine / Anita Ganeri.
   p. cm. — (Weather around you)
 Includes index.
 ISBN 0-8368-4301-0 (lib. bdg.)
 ISBN 0-8368-4306-1 (softcover)
 1. Sunshine—Juvenile literature. I. Title.
QC911.2.G36   2004
551.5'271—dc22   2004041871

This North American edition first published in 2005 by
Weekly Reader® Early Learning Library
330 West Olive Street, Suite 100
Milwaukee, WI 53212 USA

This U.S. edition copyright © 2005 by Weekly Reader® Early Learning Library. Original edition
copyright © 2004 by Hodder Wayland. First published in 2004 by Hodder Wayland, an imprint of
Hodder Children's Books, a division of Hodder Headline Limited, 338 Euston Road, London NW1 3BH, UK.

Commissioning Editor: Vicky Brooker
Book Editor: Katie Sergeant
Book Designer: Jane Hawkins
Picture Researcher: Katie Sergeant

Weekly Reader® Early Learning Library Art Direction: Tammy West
Weekly Reader® Early Learning Library Cover Design and Page Layout: Kami M. Koenig
Weekly Reader® Early Learning Library Editor: Barbara Kiely Miller

Photo Credits
The publisher would like to thank the following for permission to reproduce their photographs:
Corbis: Title page, Contents page (Craig Tuttle), 4 (Paul Barton), 6 Corbis/Digital image (original image courtesy
of NASA/CORBIS), 7 (D. Boone), 9, 13, 19 (Royalty-Free), 10 (W. Cody), 11 (Darrell Gulin), 12 (Kevin Schafer), 14 (Helen King),
15 (Tom Stewart), 16 (Gyori Antoine/Corbis Sygma), 17 (Adrian Arbib), 18 (Forestier Yves/Corbis Sygma); Corbis/Ecoscene:
20 (Chinch Gryniewicz); Corbis/Visions of America (Thomas Wiewandt): 22, 23; Getty: Cover (Stone/Martin Barraud),
5 (Stone/Donald Nausbaum); Robert Harding: 8; Science Photo Library: 21 (David Ducros).

Printed in China

1 2 3 4 5 6 7 8 9 08 07 06 05 04

Contents

A Sunny Day 4

The Sun 6

Hot and Cold 8

Plants in the Sun 10

Animals in the Sun 12

Life in the Sun 14

Heat Wave! 16

Coping with the Heat 18

Using the Sun 20

Sunshine Fact File 22

Glossary 23

Index 24

Words in **bold** can be found in the glossary on page 23.

A Sunny Day

What do you like to do on a warm and sunny day? A sunny day is perfect for a trip to the beach. Do you like to have picnics on sunny days?

Sunshine can be very strong. Sunscreen helps protect your skin. Sunglasses help keep your eyes from getting hurt. You should never look directly at the Sun.

The Sun

The Sun is far away in space. Earth's heat and light come from the Sun. The Sun keeps Earth warm enough for people, plants, and animals to live.

Heat and light travel from the Sun to Earth in lines of sunshine. The lines are called **rays**. The amount of heat that something soaks up is called its **temperature.**

Hot and Cold

Places near the **equator** are sunny and hot all year. The Sun is right above this part of Earth. The rays of sunshine there are always strong.

The top and bottom of Earth are called the poles. The poles are cold and icy all year. The Sun's rays hit the poles at a slant and are always weak.

Plants in the Sun

Plants need sunshine to make their food. They make food in their leaves. Plants mix sunshine with water from the soil and **carbon dioxide** to make food.

Farmers like sunshine because it helps their crops grow and ripen. Cold or wet weather can spoil crops. This field of barley is almost ready to **harvest**.

Animals in the Sun

Animals that live in hot places have special ways of coping. In the desert, kit foxes spend the day under the ground in their dens. Kit foxes come out at night when the air is cooler.

Camels have thick wool coats. Their coats help
keep their skin from getting a sunburn. Camels
have long legs. Their legs hold their bodies
high above the hot ground.

Life in the Sun

On a hot, sunny day, people dress in cool clothes. Some people may wear T-shirts and shorts. Many people in hot countries wear long, loose clothes. Their long clothes trap cool air inside.

In hot countries, some buildings have thick walls and small windows. Buildings with these **features** help keep out the heat. People use fans or **air conditioners** to keep cool, too.

Heat Wave!

A long time of very hot weather is called
a heat wave. The air temperature is higher
than usual. There may not be any rain.
There may not be many clouds for shade.

If there is no rain, the ground dries up. Rivers and lakes can dry out, too. People and animals get hot and thirsty. Plants droop and die.

Coping with the Heat

In a heat wave, the air can fill with fumes from cars and factories. There may be no wind to blow the fumes away. Some people find it hard to breathe.

People should drink lots of water when the weather is hot. People can get sick if their bodies cannot cool down. They can get **heatstroke**.

Using the Sun

Some people collect heat from the Sun. They put clear **solar panels** on their roofs. The solar panels are full of water. The Sun heats the water. The hot water flows into the houses through pipes and provides heat.

Sunshine is also used to run satellites.
Solar panels point at the Sun. The panels
use energy from sunlight to make electricity.

Sunshine Fact File

- The sunniest place on Earth is the eastern Sahara desert in North Africa. It gets 4,300 hours of sunshine a year. The city with the most sunshine is Yuma, Arizona. Yuma gets an amazing 4,055 hours a year!

- The highest air temperature ever recorded was 136° Fahrenheit (58° Celsius) in 1922. This temperature was recorded in Al' Aziziyah, Libya. The coldest temperature was in Vostok, Antarctica. In 1983, Vostok reached −126° F (−88° C).

- The Sun is about 93 million miles (150 million kilometers) from Earth. Sunlight zooms through space at a speed of 186,000 miles (300,000 km) a second. Sunlight only takes about 8.3 minutes to reach Earth.

Glossary

air conditioners — machines that cool buildings

carbon dioxide — a gas in the air

equator — an imaginary line around the middle of Earth

features — the parts, form, or look of something

harvest — to pick or gather crops

heatstroke — an illness caused by getting too hot. People often feel dizzy and sick.

solar panels — water-filled pipes covered by glass

rays — lines or beams, such as heat and light from the Sun

temperature — the degree of warmth or coldness of a place, substance, or person as measured on a scale

Index

air conditioners 15
animals 6, 12–13, 17

beaches 4
buildings 15

carbon dioxide 10
clothes 14
crops 11

deserts 12

Earth 6, 7, 8,
    9, 22
equator 8

fans 15

heat 6, 7, 20
heatstroke 19
heat waves 16, 17,
    18, 19

light 6, 7

plants 6, 10, 17
poles 9

rays 7, 8, 9
rivers 17

satellites 21
solar panels 20, 21
space 6, 22
sunglasses 5

temperatures 7, 16,
    22

water 10, 19, 20
weather
    cold 9, 11
    hot 8, 15, 16, 19

About the Author

Anita Ganeri is an award-winning author of children's information books. She has written many books about geography and the natural world.